I0790397

Table of Contents

Introduction

Wild boars, also known as wild pigs or Sus scrofa, are rapidly becoming one of the most significant wildlife problems facing farmers, gardeners, and homeowners. With their strong digging ability and voracious appetite, wild boars can quickly destroy crops, gardens, and farmland, causing significant financial losses and ecological damage.

Despite their growing impact, there is a lack of practical information available for effectively managing wild boars and preventing damage to property. With the aim of filling this gap, this book provides a comprehensive guide to the wild boar problem, offering practical solutions for protecting gardens and farms from these destructive pests.

"The Wild Boar Problem: Practical Solutions for Protecting Gardens and Farms" is a comprehensive guide for anyone struggling with the destructive impact of wild boars on their land. With a focus on sustainable and humane methods, this book offers practical advice and techniques for effectively deterring wild boars and preventing damage to crops, gardens, and farmlands.

Starting with a background on the biology and behavior of wild boars, this book goes on to cover a range of solutions for addressing the wild boar problem. These include physical barriers, such as fences and walls, as well as natural deterrents like planting certain shrubs and trees. The book also explores the use of non-lethal methods, such as noise and light deterrents, and humane traps for removing wild boars from your property.

Whether you are a farmer, gardener, or simply a homeowner concerned about the impact of wild boars on your land, "The Wild Boar Problem" provides the knowledge and tools you need to safeguard your property and protect your crops and gardens.

Wildboars (*Sus scrofa*) Biology and Diet

Wild Boars (Sus scrofa) are large omnivorous mammals that are native to many regions of the world, including Europe, Asia, Africa, and North America. They belong to the family Suidae, which also includes other wild pigs and domesticated pigs. Wild boars are highly adaptable animals that can survive in a variety of environments and habitats, including forests, grasslands, and agricultural lands.

Biology:

Wild boars are generally characterized by their short, sparse fur, which can range in color from black to brown, grey, or reddish. They have a large head, a short snout, and powerful jaws, which are used for foraging and digging for food. Adults typically weigh between 45 and 180 kilos, with males being larger than females. They are highly social animals that typically live in family groups, or sounders, consisting of one dominant male, several females, and their young.

Food Habits:

Wild boars are omnivores, which means they feed on a variety of plant and animal matter. They are opportunistic feeders that will consume almost anything that is available to them, including roots, bulbs, fruits, berries, nuts, insects, and small mammals. They are also known to feed on carrion, or dead animals, which can make them a significant threat to livestock and other wildlife. Wild boars are highly active and forage throughout the day and night, covering large areas in search of food.

In agricultural areas, wild boars can cause significant damage to crops and fields, as they will root around for food and can destroy entire fields of crops. This can lead to significant economic losses for farmers and landowners. In addition, their feeding habits can also contribute to soil erosion and degradation, which can have long-lasting impacts on the environment.

In natural habitats, wild boars play an important role in maintaining ecosystem health by disturbing the soil and promoting the growth of new vegetation. They also help to control the populations of other animals, such as insects, by consuming large quantities of insects and other invertebrates. However, their feeding habits can also have negative impacts on other wildlife, as they can consume or damage nests, eggs, and young of other species.

In conclusion, wild boars are complex and highly adaptable animals that play important roles in both natural and agricultural ecosystems. Understanding their biology and food habits is critical to managing their populations and reducing the impacts of their feeding habits on other wildlife and humans. Effective management strategies should aim to balance the benefits and challenges of wild boar populations in different environments, while also promoting conservation and sustainability.

Understanding their behavior

Wild Boars (Sus scrofa) are social animals that live in family groups, or sounders, consisting of one dominant male, several females, and their young. Their behavior is highly influenced by social dynamics and environmental pressures, such as hunting and the presence of stray dogs. These factors can have significant impacts on wild boar populations and their behavior, affecting their distribution, migration patterns, and overall well-being.

Behavior:

Wild boars are highly active and forage throughout the day and night, covering large areas in search of food. They are known for their strong social bonds, with mothers forming close relationships with their young, and adult males forming dominance hierarchies within their sounders. Wild boars are also highly vocal animals, communicating through grunts, snorts, and barks to maintain social bonds and warn of potential threats.

Hunting Pressure:

Hunting has been a significant source of pressure for wild boar populations for centuries, with populations being hunted for their meat, hide, and tusks. Hunting can have a significant impact on wild boar behavior, as it can disrupt social structures, alter migration patterns, and lead to increased stress levels and changes in feeding behavior. Additionally, hunting can lead to the removal of dominant males, which can disrupt social hierarchies and result in increased aggression and territorial behavior in surviving males.

In some regions, hunting pressure has also led to the development of a 'wariness' trait, with wild boars becoming more cautious and elusive in the presence of humans. This can make them more difficult to manage and control, as they are less likely to respond to traditional management strategies.

Stray Dog Pressure:

The presence of stray dogs can also have significant impacts on wild boar behavior and populations. Stray dogs can compete with wild boars for food, leading to changes in feeding patterns and territory use. Additionally, stray dogs can also pose a threat to wild boars, leading to increased stress levels and changes in behavior. In some cases, wild boars may even alter their migration patterns to avoid areas with high populations of stray dogs.

In conclusion, the behavior of wild boars is highly influenced by both hunting pressure and the presence of stray dogs. These factors can have significant impacts on wild boar populations and their behavior, affecting their distribution, migration patterns, and overall well-being. Effective management strategies should aim to balance the impacts of hunting and stray dogs on wild boar populations, while also promoting conservation and sustainability. This may involve adjusting hunting regulations, managing stray dog populations, and implementing non-lethal management strategies to reduce the impacts of these pressures on wild boar behavior and populations.

Physical Barriers for wildboars

There are several physical barriers that can be used to prevent wild boars from accessing crops, gardens, and farmland. Some of the most effective methods include:

1. **Electric fences**: Electric fences are highly effective in keeping wild boars away, as they provide a physical barrier that is difficult for the animals to penetrate. The fences work by delivering a mild shock when an animal comes into contact with them, deterring them from entering the protected area.

2. **Perimeter fences**: Perimeter fences can be used to enclose gardens, farms, and other areas, keeping wild boars out. They can be made from a variety of materials, including wood, wire mesh, or plastic, and can be designed to be either permanent or temporary.

3. **Raised garden beds**: Raised garden beds can prevent wild boars from digging up crops and destroying gardens. By elevating the soil and plants, they make it difficult for the animals to access the roots and stems of plants.

4. **Barriers made from natural materials**: Barriers made from natural materials, such as rocks, boulders, or plants, can also be used to prevent wild boars from accessing crops and gardens. These barriers can provide

a physical barrier while also blending in with the natural landscape.

5. **Livestock guards**: Livestock guards, such as dogs or donkeys, can be used to protect crops and gardens from wild boars. These animals can be trained to deter wild boars by barking, charging, or chasing them away from the protected area.

Each of these methods has its own advantages and disadvantages, and the best solution will depend on the specific needs and circumstances of the property being protected. By using a combination of physical barriers and other management techniques, farmers, gardeners, and homeowners can effectively protect their land from the damaging impact of wild boars.

Here are the advantages and disadvantages of each physical barrier:

1. **Electric Fences:**

   Advantages:

   - Highly effective in deterring wild boars
   - Can be quickly installed and removed

- Can be used to protect a variety of different areas, including gardens, farms, and other property

- Can be powered by solar panels, making them a more environmentally friendly option

Disadvantages:

- May require regular maintenance

- Can be expensive to purchase and install

- Can be dangerous to wildlife and humans if not properly maintained

- May need to be periodically adjusted to accommodate changes in the landscape

2. Perimeter Fences:

Advantages:

- Provide a physical barrier that is difficult for wild boars to penetrate

- Can be made from a variety of materials, making them customizable to suit the needs of the property

- Can be used to protect large areas, such as farms or ranches

Disadvantages:

- Can be expensive to purchase and install

- May require regular maintenance to keep the fence in good condition

- May be visually unappealing in certain landscapes

- May not be suitable for smaller properties or gardens

3. Raised Garden Beds:

Advantages:

- Protect crops and gardens from wild boars by elevating the soil and plants

- Can be aesthetically pleasing, adding visual interest to the landscape

- Can be relatively inexpensive to construct

Disadvantages:

- May not be suitable for all types of crops

- Can be difficult to access for maintenance or harvest

- May not be suitable for properties with limited space

4. Barriers Made from Natural Materials:

Advantages:

- Blend in with the natural landscape, making them a visually appealing option

- Can be relatively inexpensive to construct

- Can provide additional habitat for wildlife

- May not require regular maintenance

Disadvantages:

- May not be as effective as other methods in deterring wild boars

- Can be difficult to install in certain landscapes

- May not be suitable for large areas or properties with limited space

5. Livestock Guards:

Advantages:

- Can be highly effective in deterring wild boars

- Can provide additional benefits, such as guarding against other wildlife or providing companionship

- Can be relatively inexpensive compared to other methods

Disadvantages:

- Can be difficult to train and manage

- May require regular care and maintenance

- May not be suitable for all properties, especially those with limited space

- May not be an option in certain locations, such as urban areas.

It's important to note that each property and situation is unique, and the best solution will depend on a variety of factors, including the size and layout of the property, the presence of other wildlife, and the property owner's specific needs and preferences. By carefully considering the advantages and disadvantages of each option, property owners can choose the physical barrier that best suits their needs and effectively protect their land from wild boars.

Natural Deterrents

Here are some natural deterrents that can be used to protect against wild boars and the advantages and disadvantages of each:

1. **Plants:**

   Advantages:

   - Can provide a visually appealing and natural solution to deterring wild boars

   - Certain plants, such as prickly shrubs or trees, can physically deter wild boars

   - Can provide additional benefits, such as providing food or habitat for wildlife

   Disadvantages:

   - May not be effective in all situations, depending on the size and strength of the wild boar population

   - May require regular maintenance and pruning to remain effective

   - May not be suitable for all types of landscapes or climates

2. Noise:

Advantages:

- Can be an effective deterrent for wild boars
- Can be relatively inexpensive to implement
- May not require regular maintenance

Disadvantages:

- May not be effective in all situations, as wild boars may eventually become habituated to the noise
- Can be disruptive to other wildlife and humans
- May not be suitable for all types of landscapes or climates

3. Light:

Advantages:

- Can be an effective deterrent for wild boars, especially when used in combination with noise
- Can be relatively inexpensive to implement
- May not require regular maintenance

Disadvantages:

- May not be effective in all situations, as wild boars may eventually become habituated to the light

- Can be disruptive to other wildlife and humans

- May not be suitable for all types of landscapes or climates

4. Scents:

Advantages:

- Certain scents, such as human or predator scents, can effectively deter wild boars

- Can be relatively inexpensive to implement

- May not require regular maintenance

Disadvantages:

- May not be effective in all situations, as wild boars may eventually become habituated to the scent

- Can be difficult to obtain and apply the correct scent

- Can be disruptive to other wildlife and humans

- May not be suitable for all types of landscapes or climates.

It's important to note that the effectiveness of natural deterrents can vary depending on the size and strength of the wild boar population, as well as other factors such as the size and layout of the property and the presence of other wildlife. As with physical barriers, property owners should carefully consider the advantages and disadvantages of each option before choosing the best natural deterrent for their needs.

Non-lethal Methods

Here are some non-lethal methods that can be used to protect against wild boars and the advantages and disadvantages of each:

1. **Habitat modification:**

   Advantages:

   - Can effectively reduce the number of wild boars in the area

   - Can provide additional benefits, such as improving wildlife habitat or reducing soil erosion

   - May be more sustainable and humane than other methods

   Disadvantages:

   - Can be time-consuming and expensive to implement

   - May require regular maintenance to remain effective

   - May not be suitable for all types of landscapes or climates

2. Repellents:

Advantages:

- Can be an effective and humane way to deter wild boars
- Can be relatively inexpensive to implement
- May not require regular maintenance

Disadvantages:

- May not be effective in all situations, as wild boars may eventually become habituated to the repellent
- Can be difficult to obtain and apply the correct repellent
- Can be disrupted by environmental factors, such as rain or strong winds
- May not be suitable for all types of landscapes or climates

3. Fencing:

Advantages:

- Can effectively deter wild boars from entering the protected area
- Can provide additional benefits, such as improving wildlife habitat or reducing soil erosion

- May be relatively inexpensive to implement

Disadvantages:

- Can be time-consuming and expensive to construct
- May require regular maintenance to remain effective
- May not be suitable for all types of landscapes or climates

4. Traps and relocation:

Advantages:

- Can effectively remove wild boars from the area
- Can provide additional benefits, such as reducing the overall population size
- May be more sustainable and humane than other methods

Disadvantages:

- Can be time-consuming and expensive to implement
- May require specialized training and equipment
- May not be suitable for all types of landscapes or climates
- Can be illegal in certain jurisdictions.

It's important to note that the effectiveness of non-lethal methods can vary depending on the size and strength of the wild boar population, as well as other factors such as the size and layout of the property and the presence of other wildlife. Property owners should carefully consider the advantages and disadvantages of each option before choosing the best non-lethal method for their needs.

Humane Removal Techniques

Here are some humane removal techniques that can be used to protect against wild boars and the advantages and disadvantages of each:

1. **Traps and relocation:**

    Advantages:

    - Can effectively remove wild boars from the area

    - Can provide additional benefits, such as reducing the overall population size

    - May be more sustainable and humane than other methods

    Disadvantages:

    - Can be time-consuming and expensive to implement

    - May require specialized training and equipment

    - May not be suitable for all types of landscapes or climates

    - Can be illegal in certain jurisdictions.

    - There is a risk of injury to the captured wild boar during the trapping and relocation process.

2. Fertility control:

Advantages:

- Can effectively reduce the wild boar population over time

- May be more sustainable and humane than other methods

- Can provide additional benefits, such as reducing the overall population size

Disadvantages:

- Can be time-consuming and expensive to implement

- May require specialized training and equipment

- May not be suitable for all types of landscapes or climates

- Can be difficult to obtain and apply the correct fertility control method

3. Shooting:

Advantages:

- Can effectively remove wild boars from the area

- May be less expensive than other methods

- Can provide additional benefits, such as reducing the overall population size

Disadvantages:

- May not be suitable for all types of landscapes or climates

- Can be illegal in certain jurisdictions

- May require specialized training and equipment

- There is a risk of injury or death to the shooter and other individuals

Note from the author: Shooting and Hunting should be the least available method that will be used.

It's important to note that the effectiveness of humane removal techniques can vary depending on the size and strength of the wild boar population, as well as other factors such as the size and layout of the property and the presence of other wildlife. Property owners should carefully consider the advantages and disadvantages of each option before choosing the best humane removal method for their needs. Additionally, it's important to follow all local laws and regulations regarding wildlife removal, as some methods may be illegal in certain areas.

DIY – Cheap solution with red-white tape

Guide to Using Red-White Tape to Protect Gardens from Wild Boars

Wild boars can be a destructive force in gardens, causing significant damage to crops and plants. Fortunately, there is an effective and affordable solution to deter wild boars: red-white tape. Here is a step-by-step guide to setting up and using red-white tape to protect your garden from wild boars.

Materials needed:

- Red-white tape (available at most hardware stores)

- Posts or stakes

- Hammer or post driver

Step 1: Determine the boundaries of your garden Decide which areas of your garden you want to protect from wild boars and mark the boundaries with stakes or flags.

Step 2: Install posts or stakes around the perimeter of your garden Using a hammer or post driver, install posts or stakes around the perimeter of your garden at intervals of 50-80 cm. Make sure the posts or stakes are firmly in the ground.

Step 3: Attach the red-white tape to the posts or stakes Cut lengths of red-white tape and attach them to the posts or stakes using clips or ties. The red and white stripes should be facing outwards, towards the garden.

Step 4: Adjust the height of the tape Make sure the tape is at a height that will be visible to wild boars. Usually, a height of 50-60 cm is sufficient.

Step 5: Monitor and maintain the tape Regularly inspect the tape to make sure it is still securely attached to the posts or stakes. Replace any tape that has become damaged or detached.

Step 6: Enjoy your protected garden Wild boars have an innate fear of moving, contrasting stripes and will typically avoid gardens protected by red-white tape. With this simple and affordable solution, you can protect your

Beware: Red-white tape is a short term solution up to 3 months without be destroyed, and that timeline depends on the weather conditions.

Conclusion

In conclusion, wild boars can cause significant damage to gardens and farms, leading to reduced crop yields and increased costs for farmers and gardeners. However, with effective management strategies, it is possible to minimize these impacts and reduce conflicts between wild boars and human populations.

The most effective solutions for protecting gardens and farms from wild boars will depend on the specific circumstances of each situation. Physical barriers, such as fences, can provide effective protection in many cases, while humane removal techniques can be used to safely relocate problem individuals.

Additionally, the impacts of hunting pressure and stray dogs on wild boar behavior should also be considered in management strategies. Effective management may involve adjusting hunting regulations, managing stray dog populations, and implementing non-lethal management strategies to reduce the impacts of these pressures on wild boar behavior and populations.

Ultimately, the goal of wild boar management should be to minimize conflicts between wild boars and human populations, while also preserving wild boars as an important component of our natural heritage. With the right tools and techniques, it is possible to achieve this goal and protect our gardens and farms from the impacts of wild boars.